MISSOURI

A Picture Book to Remember Her by

CRESCENT BOOKS
NEW YORK

CLB 872
© 1986 Illustrations and text: Colour Library Books Ltd.,
   Guildford, Surrey, England.
Text filmsetting by Acesetters Ltd., Richmond, Surrey, England.
Printed and bound in Barcelona. Spain by Cronion, S.A.
1986 edition published by Crescent Books, distributed by Crown Publishers, Inc.
ISBN 0 517 47792 0
h g f e d c b a

In the 1860s, when Missouri was still young, the Secretary of State, William Seward, said: "I see here one state that is capable of assuming the great trust of being the middle man, the mediator, the common center between the Pacific and the Atlantic.

It is right in the middle, and the symbolism of St. Louis as an Eastern city and Kansas City as the spot where the West begins is not something to take lightly. The fact that the two cities are connected by the navigable Missouri River, and that it joins the Mississippi at its half-way point on Missouri's eastern border, makes Seward's remarks seem almost too obvious.

The Ozark Mountains spill over into Missouri from Arkansas, and the people fit the same image as their neighbors to the south; that of being slightly backward backwoods folks who are a little suspicious of other folks who come to see their beautiful hills.

Oddly, they are less "Southern" in their outlook on life than the people who settled the extreme northern part of Missouri, where they still call an amalgam of counties "Little Dixie," though the countryside has more in common with nearby Iowa than any Southern state. On the other hand, there is a little bump of territory in Missouri's southeast corner that looks more like the common vision of Dixie than most parts of Dixie itself.

The people of Missouri came from all sections of the Eastern and Southern United States, but most of them agree that being a Missourian requires a very special quality. They call it "cussedness."

Most of their great-grandparents came from the Deep South on their way north and west in search of independence from the societies established in their home states in the 17th century. Like the immigrants who poured into the Northeast from Europe, they were looking for a new life, but they already had a tradition of independence and wouldn't settle for anything less than allowing the tradition to grow. In the 20th century, we'd call them radicals, or at the very least "nonconformists," but their contemporaries called them "ornery."

It all became intensified during the Civil War, when the state was divided and fought on both sides, often on its own soil. In the end, the orneryness was manifested as suspicion and ever since, no self-respecting Missourian will accept any idea at face value, challenging instead to "show me!"

What they've shown the rest of us is people like Harry Truman and Mark Twain, Casey Stengel and Dale Carnegie. They've shown us better blues singers, the joys of a corn cob pipe and the Spirit of St. Louis. They've shown the way west to thousands, but they also showed thousands that once you're in Missouri, there's no need to go anywhere else.

Facing page: the Gateway Arch.

St. Louis. Left: city center. Above: Market Street. Top: the Old Courthouse. Overleaf: the Mississippi River with insets: (top left) the Busch Memorial Stadium; (bottom left) paddle steamers and (right) the Old Courthouse.

St. Louis. Above: the Basilica of St. Louis, King of France, more commonly referred to as the Old Cathedral. It was built in 1831 to replace the original log structure of the 1770s. Top: a cobblestoned street in the shadow of the Gateway Arch. Right and inset top right: the sternwheeler *Tom Sawyer* on the Mississippi.

St. Louis. Left: the Busch Memorial Stadium. Above: the ornate interior of the Fox Theater. Top: the airy, modern interior of the St. Louis Center. Overleaf: (top left, bottom left and top right) the Gateway Arch and (bottom right) a stern-wheeler on the Mississippi.

St. Louis. Above: *The Runner* in front of the Old Courthouse. Opened in 1845, the Old Courthouse was for many years the main feature of the city skyline and served as a landmark for the riverboats which plied the Mississippi. Today, two of the original courthouses remain and the whole buildng has been renovated to its original condition. Right: the 12-acre Busch Memorial Stadium, which can hold 50,000 spectators.

Top left and top right: scenes from the Black Madonna Shrine at Eureka. Left: the First State Capitol in St. Charles, which has been restored to its 1821 condition. Above: the restored MKT Depot, St. Charles. Facing page: (top) the St. Charles Town Hall and (bottom) St. Charles County Courthouse.

Here stood the board fence which Tom Sawyer persuaded his gang to pay him for the privilege of whitewashing. Tom sat by and saw that it was well done.

TOM SAWYER'S FENCE

Hannibal. Above: the Mark Twain Museum. Top: the boyhood home of Samuel Langhorne Clemens, better known as Mark Twain. Right: the lighthouse on Cardiff Hill. Facing page: the statue of Tom Sawyer and Huckleberry Finn, Cardiff Hill.

Facing page: (top) the Mississippi near Hannibal and (bottom) the Mark Twain State Park. Top: the Rockcliffe Mansion and (above) the Garth Woodside Mansion, Hannibal. Left: the Mississippi.

Below: a ruined farmhouse. Right: a pecan nut farmer, Brunswick. Bottom: corn harvesting. Facing page: a tobacco-curing barn near Weston and (bottom) cattle farming. Overleaf: grain field near Weston with insets; (top left) storage warehouse and (right) aging whiskey, both at the McCormick Distillery near Weston.

Kansas City. Top: the arched windows mark the Union Station, which opened in 1914 and once accommodated 200 trains daily. Above: the limestone Liberty Memorial, dedicated to the dead of World War I. Remaining pictures: the City Center.

Kansas City. Left: the Vaille Mansion. Bottom: Kansas City Museum, which concentrates on science, natural history and local history. Below and facing page: Country Club Plaza, an area of quality shops and boutiques in elegant surroundings.

KANSAS CITY MUSEUM OF HISTORY AND SCIENCE

KANSAS CITY MUSEUM

Kansas City recalls its sister city, Seville in Spain, at the Country Club Plaza: (facing page, bottom) the Giralda Tower and (above) a fountain, both inspired by originals in the Spanish city.

Kansas City. Right and top: statuary at the Country Club Plaza. Top right: the Stockyards. Above: the Nelson Gallery of Art. Facing page: scenes from the City Market, which is centered around 5th Street.

Kansas City. Top: the Stockyards. Left and above: stadia at the Harry S. Truman Sports Complex, which can seat 119,000 spectators simultaneously. Facing page: the city center.

This page: Independence. Below: Independence Square. Right: McCoy House. Bottom left: Independence Station. Bottom right: the Bingham-Waggoner Home of 1855. Facing page: Johnson County's Old Courthouse in Warrensburg.

JOHNSON COUNTY'S
OLD COURTHOUSE
1838-1871

Here in 1870, George Graham
Vest delivered his Eulogy to
the Dog in the Old Drum Case.

The building served as a seat
of Justice, a meetinghouse, and
vital record keeper in the
county's formative years. It was the scene of a
murder, Civil War troop occupation, and a
daring raid that removed and hid the records
for three years.

It is one of the rare examples of Federal
style architecture this far West.

JOHNSON COUNTY HISTORICAL SOCIETY, 1976
GIFT OF CENTENNIAL CLUB, MFWC

On the sign:

FORT OSAGE

✶ ✶ ✶

ON THE FIRST EXPLORATION
TO THE PACIFIC IN 1804 LEWIS
AND CLARK NAMED THIS SITE
FORT POINT AND IN 1808 WILLIAM
CLARK RETURNED TO BUILD A
FORTIFIED TRADING POST TO WIN
THE INDIANS FROM SPANISH AND
BRITISH INFLUENCE. IT WAS
OPERATED BY THE UNITED STATES
UNTIL 1822.

FORT OSAGE PLAYED AN ACTIVE
AND IMPORTANT PART IN THE
EARLIEST DEVELOPMENT OF THE
LOUISIANA PURCHASE BY THE
MISSOURI RIVER AND ROCKY
MOUNTAIN FUR TRADE AND THE
PLAINS TRADE WITH MEXICO.

Top left: Watkin's Mill, near Lawson.
Above and top right: the completely
rebuilt Fort Osage, first constructed
in 1808. Right: the view from Fort
Osage. Facing page: a pumpkin figure,
near Sibley.

POSTED
PRIVATE PROPERT
HUNTING, FISHING, TRA
TRESPASSING FOR AN
IS ST

Facing page and top: Jesse Hall and (above) the Columns, University of Missouri, Columbia. Left: Winston Churchill Memorial, Fulton. Overleaf: the State Capitol, Jefferson City.

Jefferson City. Facing page: the Governor's Mansion of 1871. Top and left: the State Capitol, built in 1917. Above: the statue commemorating the signing of the Louisiana Purchase.

Facing page: the Lake of the Ozarks near Bagnell Dam. Top: the Ravenswood House near Tipton. Left: Burger's Smokehouse, California, the largest producer of natural hams in the nation.

These pages: the beautiful formations of the Meramec Caverns near Stanton, where Jesse James was once besieged by a posse from Gadshill. Overleaf: the Onondaga Caves near Leasburg.

Top left and overleaf left: Alley
Springs Mill. Top right: Falling
Springs Mill. Left: Dawt Mill. Above:
Current River. Facing page: Rockbridge
Mill. Overleaf right: Dillard Mill.

Previous pages: (left) Hodgson Mill;
(top right) Appleton Mill and (bottom
right) Ballinger Mill. Above: Elephant
Rocks State Park. Top: Red Bluffs, at
Davisville. Right: Rocky Falls. Facing
page: (top) Alley Springs and (bottom)
Dawt Mill.

Above and right: Ray House at Wilson's Creek National Battlefield. Center: John Q. Hammonds Fountains and (top) modern buildings, both in Springfield.

Top: Jasper County Courthouse,
Carthage. Above: the *Praying Hands*
statue, Joplin. Right: Grand Falls.
Facing page: Table Rock State Park.
Overleaf: Table Rock Dam.

160